Are pleased to be associated with

'A Little Bit of Paradise'

DEEP BAY, ANTIGUA

TEL: (809) 462 1801

Hansib Publishing would like to thank the following companies without whose commitment and support this book would not have been possible.

Antigua-Barbuda Social Security Board
PO Box 1125, St. John's, Antigua
Tel: 462-1315/1317/0446/0644
Cable Address 'SOCES'

Antigua Catering Services Ltd
V.C. Bird International Airport,
PO Box 585, Antigua
Tel: (809) 462-3121/3122
Telex: AK 2123

Antigua Public Utilities Authority
PO Box 416, Telephone House
Long Street, St. John's, Antigua
Tel: 462-1000

Admiral's Inn
Nelson Dockyard
PO Box 713, St. John's, Antigua
Tel: (809) 463-1027 (from Abroad)
     (809) 463-1534 (Inland)
Cable ADMIRALS

The Anchorage Hotel
Dickenson Bay
PO Box 147, St. John's Antigua
Tel: (809) 462-0267/2512

Antigua Commercial Bank
PO Box 95, St Mary's Street,
St John's, Antigua
Tel: (809) 462-1217/8/9 462-2085

Joseph Benjamin Ltd
PO Box 563, Redcliffe Street,
St. John's, Antigua
Tel: (809) 462-0733/0154/0932
Telex: 2145 CWTX AGY AK
Cable "BENJIES" Antigua

Blue Waters Beach Hotel
PO Box 256, St. John's, Antigua
Tel: (809) 462-0290/0292
Telex: 2066 BLU WTR AK
Fax: (809) 462-0293

British-American Insurance
Company Ltd
PO Box 36, Redcliffe Street,
St. John's, Antigua
Tel: (809) 462-1143

Cable & Wireless (West Indies) Ltd
(incorporated in England)
PO Box 65, 42/44 St. Mary's Street,
St. John's, Antigua
Tel: (809) 462-0840
Telex: AK 2149

Carib Aviation
Charter Airline
PO Box 318, St. John's, Antigua
Tel: (809) 462-3147/3125

Charles Electrical & Household
Gigi Plaza, cnr. Market & Nevis Sts.
PO Box 1256, St. John's, Antigua
Tel: 462-1040

Crabbs Slipway and Marina Ltd
Box 271, St. John's, Antigua
Tel: (809) 463 2113

Curtain Bluff Hotel
PO Box 288, St. John's, Antigua
Tel: (809) 463 1115/6/7

Joseph Dew
Division of Dantzler – West Indies Ltd
(incorporated in Nassau, Bahamas)
PO Box 126, St. John's Antigua
Tel: (809) 462 1210
Cable Address: DEW, Antigua
Telex: 2125 DEWDANT AK

The East Caribbean Group
Campden Park Bay, PO Box 612,
St, Vincent & The Grenadines
Tel: (809) 457 1918
Telex: 7537 ECFM LTD VQ
Facsimile: (809) 457 7533

Halcyon Cove Beach Resort & Casino
PO Box 251, St. John's Antigua
Tel: (809) 462-0256
Telex: 2137 HALCOVE AK

Half Moon Bay Hotel
PO Box 144, St. John's, Antigua
Tel: (809) 463-2101/2
Telex: 2138 JOHNANJO AK
ANTIGUA W.I.
HALFMOON
Cable HALFMOON

Harmony Hall
Brown Bay Mill nr. Freetown, Antigua
Art Gallery, Gift Shop, Restaurant & Pub
Tel: (809) 463-2057

Joseph's Supermarket
& Trucking Service
PO Box 1136, Antigua

Jumby Bay Club
PO Box 243, Long Island, Antigua
Tel: (809) 462-6000
Telex: 2092 JUMBAY AK

Leeward Motors Limited
P.O. Box 101, Old Parham Road
St. John's, Antigua
Phone: (809) 462 1555
Cable: CARPORT

LIAT (1974) Ltd
V.C. Bird International Airport
PO Box 819, St. John's, Antigua
Tel: (809) 642 0700

Lolita's
PO Box 658, Market Street,
St. John's, Antigua
Tel: 462-1186

Joseph   Michael Holdings Ltd
P O Box 136, St. John's, Antigua
Tel: (809) 462 1142/3244
Cable: JOEMIKES

New England International
Development Corporation
32 Elm Street,
PO Box 1629
New Haven
CT 06506 U.S.A.

Pigott Lumber and Hardware Co
Box 271 American Road,
St. John's, Antigua
Tel: (809) 462 4870/1

Mannuel Preud'Homme
Long Bay
Dian Point
St. John's, Antigua
Tel: (809) 462 2050
Telex: 2065 ABC PROM

The Royal Antiguan
A Savoy Resort,
Deep Bay, Antigua
Tel: (809) 462 1801
USA (800) 223 1588/(212) 661 4540
Canada (800) 531 6767

St. James Club Antigua Ltd
PO Box 63, St. John's, Antigua
Tel: (809) 463 1430 or 1113
Telex: 2088 STJ CLUB AK

Sealy Mattress C. (Antigua) Ltd
Coolidge Industrial Estate
PO Box 1158, St. John's Antigua
Tel: (809) 462-1541/3231/1536
Cable "SEAMATCO"

Ian P Shoul
PO Box 102, St John's
Antigua
Tel: (809) 462-1139/1140
Cable "SINGER" Antigua.

State Insurance Corporation
Government of Antigua
PO Box 290, St. John's, Antigua
Tel: 462-0110/0114/3945
Telegram 2177 SIDAN AK

Sun Images (Caribbean) Ltd
PO Box 1159, Coolidge,
St. John's, Antigua
Tel: (809) 462 4320

Swiss-American Bank Ltd
PO Box 230, Redcliffe Street?
St. John's, Antigua
Tel: (809) 462-4460/1/2/3/4
Telex: 2181 SA BANK

West Indies Oil Company Ltd
(incorporated in Antigua)
PO Box 230, Friars Hill,
St. John's, Antigua
Tel: (809) 462 0140/1/2/3/4

First published in 1988 by Hansib Publishing Limited,
Tower House, 139/149 Fonthill Road,
London N4 3HF, England.
Tel: 01-281 1191. Fax: 01-263 9656

All photographs taken by Allan Aflak

Cover: A beach near Crab Hill on the
south-west coast of Antigua.

Design, typesetting and production by
Hansib Publishing Limited.

Printed and bound in Great Britain by
William Clowes Ltd, Beccles & London.

Colour reproduction by Hilo Offset.

ISBN 1-870518-09-8

A Little Bit of Paradise

Antigua & Barbuda

Acknowledgements

(Opposite) National flag of Antigua and Barbuda

The production of this book would not have been possible without the help and support of many organisations and individuals in Antigua and Barbuda as well as other countries.

We would like to express our appreciation and thanks to:

Deputy Prime Minister Lester Bird who originally commissioned the project and Minister Hugh Marshall who supported it on its initiation as well as later;

Alan Aflak whose photographic efforts and endeavours far exceeded our not undemanding expectations. Not only did he shoot with a camera for 18 months – he also learnt scuba diving in order to take the underwater shots, went flying to take the aerial shots and took to the sea to capture the islands in their setting;

Ron Sanders, the former High Commissioner to London, whose rich knowledge of Antigua and Barbuda and whose advice we availed ourselves of on many occasions. The historical photos used in the book are from Ron Sanders' archives;

Bobby Reis, Ariana, Elfreda and Milton of Sun Images for the facilities they made available – facilities that we continue to abuse with no plans to stop;

Makeda Mikael and all at the Ministry of Foreign Affairs; The management and staff of the Anchorage and Halcyon Hotels, who have always been very kind and co-operative during our numerous visits;

All the businesses and individuals who have greatly helped by ordering advance copies of the book;

Coral Bailey and Geraldine Taylor of British Airways who may have lost patience at our constant cancellations and rebookings but never let us know it;

John Nicholls and Jennifer Hill of William Clowes Printers who kept their cool whilst waiting for elusive photographs;

Naomi Marshall for continuing support;

Abi Ries who kept us mobile – as did the taxi drivers;

My colleagues at Hansib, particularly John St Lewis, John Hughes, Keith Bennett and Michelle Wilson;

My son Kash who put in an enormous amount of work on this project alongside many others;

The numerous other friends and helpers.

To all of you – many thanks.

Preface

(Opposite) National emblem of Antigua and Barbuda

The publication of *A Little Bit of Paradise* represents a culmination of an increasingly successful relationship between our publishing house and the government, businesses and people of Antigua and Barbuda.

During 1986 we were commissioned to produce a special supplement to mark the fifth anniversary of national independence and in the course of this work I was invited to the home of Deputy Prime Minister Lester Bird. He showed me a richly illustrated book depicting another Caribbean state with a view to finding out if we could produce something of comparable quality. When I assured him that we could actually do better the Deputy Prime Minister requested me to undertake the project, whilst stressing that it would be free from government funding. The Deputy Prime Minister and myself were agreed that if the initial funding could be arranged then the potential sales would more than justify the initial investment.

However, production costs on a book of this quality are so high that we decided to appeal to the Antigua business community for their support in the form of advance orders. The response was such that the project was able to go ahead.

To the extent that this book will prove invaluable for visitors to Antigua and Barbuda and will encourage others to visit then we trust that this initial vote of confidence will not have been misplaced.

The work involved in preparing *A Little Bit of Paradise* gave me the opportunity of travelling widely throughout the country during the different seasons of the year and it is my hope that the inspiration that I have felt at different times has come to be reflected not only in an excellent pictorial album but also in a work that will educate and inspire.

Having had dealings with people from all walks of life from Prime Minister Vere Bird through to people in the smallest village and on the most tranquil beach, I feel confident in addressing a few words to the people of Antigua and Barbuda. You should be proud of the realities of your country particularly when they are compared with those in some other countries of the region. Tourism, of course, plays a major role in the national economy and so it is important to adopt a correct perspective on it. Some of our people feel that there is a certain stigma attached to the

EACH ENDEAVOURING. ALL ACHIEVING

industry and that to work in it is akin to a type of servitude.

Nothing could be further from the truth. It is by no means only our Caribbean peoples that depend on tourism as a mainstay of the economy. Britain and the United States of America, as well as, to a somewhat lesser extent, the Soviet Union and other socialist countries, make enormous efforts to attract tourism, not least because it is a major provider of foreign exchange. Work in the tourism sector must therefore be seen as work for the betterment of the country and not be viewed solely from the perspective of its not unattractive salaries.

All those who have visited Antigua and Barbuda have enjoyed its beauty and its beaches. It is said that Antigua has more beaches than there are days in the year – but with such numbers who's counting? The beauty and beaches are by no means the country's only attractions. From experience I know that it has excellent travel and telecommunications facilities. But more important than any material facility is the spirit of the people manifested in their gaiety, optimism, pride and hospitality. This is Antigua and Barbuda's greatest resource.

If you have already had the pleasure of visiting Antigua and Barbuda this aptly titled book will serve to periodically refresh your memory. If you have yet to visit the country we would just like to point out that you do not have to take our word – the little bit of paradise will always welcome visitors.

Arif Ali,
St John's,
Antigua, 1988

(Opposite) V.C. Bird International Airport, Antigua

(Bottom) Supersonic Concorde in Antigua

8

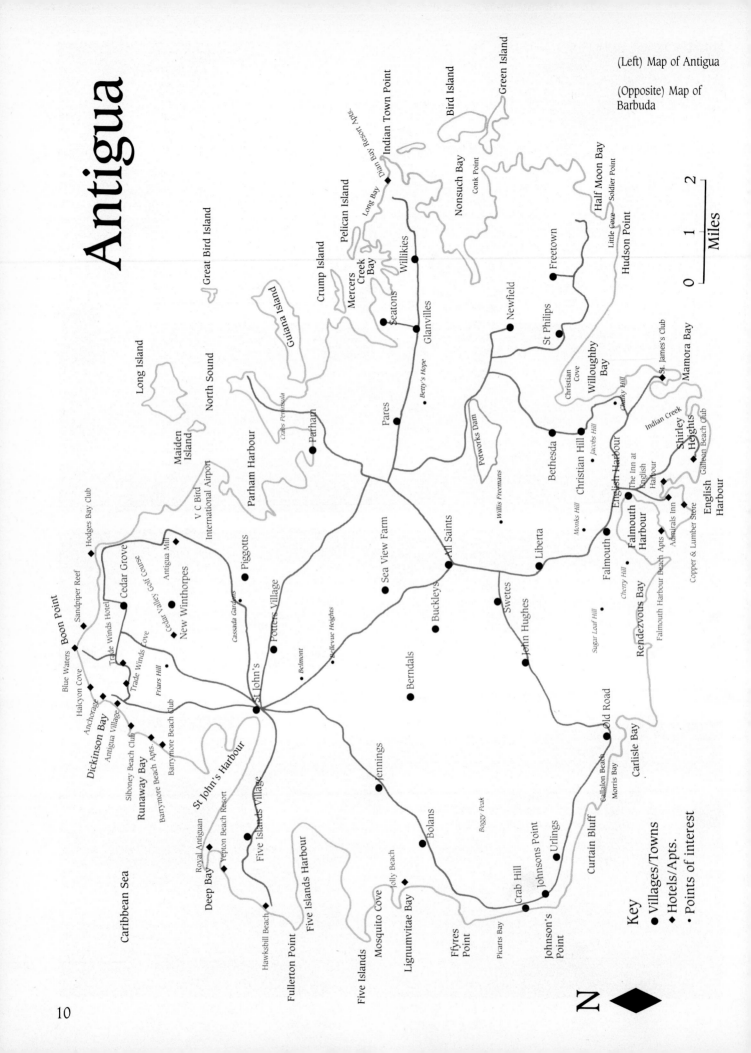

Antigua

(Left) Map of Antigua

(Opposite) Map of Barbuda

Caribbean Sea

Great Bird Island

Long Island

North Sound

Maiden Island

Guiana Island

Crump Island

Pelican Island

Mercers Creek Bay

Indian Town Point

Long Bay

Dian Bay Resort Apts.

Bird Island

Green Island

Nonsuch Bay

Conk Point

Half Moon Bay

Soldier Point

Little Cove

Hudson Point

Freetown

St Philips

Newfield

Willikies

Seatons

Glanvilles

Betty's Hope

Pares

Parham Harbour

Parham

Crabs Peninsula

Potworks Dam

Christian Cove

Willoughby Bay

St. James's Club

Mamora Bay

Indian Creek

Shirley Heights

Galleon Beach Club

English Harbour

Cherry Hill

Bethesda

Christian Hill

Jacobs Hill

Monks Hill

Willis Freemans

The Inn at English Harbour

Admirals Inn

Copper & Lumber Store

English Harbour

Falmouth Harbour

Falmouth

Cherry Hill

Falmouth Harbour Beach Apts.

Liberta

Rendezvous Bay

Boon Point

Hodges Bay Club

Sandpiper Reef

Blue Waters

Halcyon Cove

Anchorage

Antigua Village

Dickinson Bay

Siboney Beach Club

Runaway Bay

Barrymore Beach Apts.

Barrymore Beach Club

Trade Winds Hotel

Trade Winds Cove

Friars Hill

Cedar Grove

Antigua Mill

Cedar Valley Golf Course

V C Bird International Airport

New Winthorpes

Piggotts

Cassada Gardens

St John's

Potters Village

Belmont

Bellevue Heights

Sea View Farm

All Saints

Buckleys

Berndals

Swetes

John Hughes

Sugar Loaf Hill

Old Road

Callalon Beach

Morris Bay

Carlisle Bay

Curtain Bluff

Crab Hill

Johnsons Point

Urlings

Johnson's Point

Picarts Bay

Boggy Peak

Bolans

Ffyres Point

Jolly Beach

Mosquito Cove

Lignumvitae Bay

Jennings

Five Islands

Fullerton Point

Five Islands Harbour

Hawksbill Beach

Deep Bay

Yepton Beach Resort

Royal Antiguan

Five Islands Village

St John's Harbour

Key
● Villages/Towns
◆ Hotels/Apts.
• Points of interest

N

Miles

0   1   2

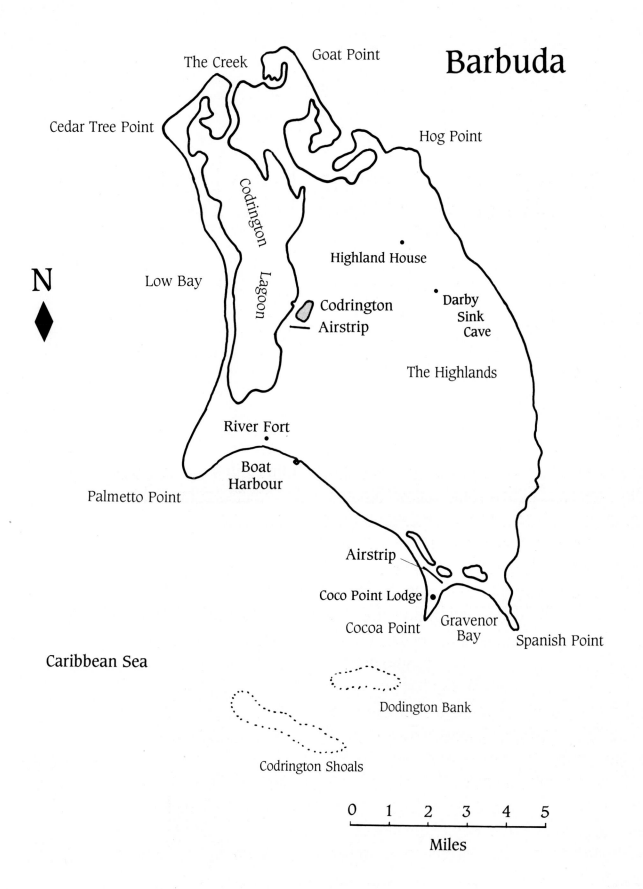

Barbuda

The Creek   Goat Point

Cedar Tree Point

Hog Point

Codrington Lagoon

Highland House

N

Low Bay

Codrington
Airstrip

Darby
Sink
Cave

The Highlands

River Fort

Boat
Harbour

Palmetto Point

Airstrip

Coco Point Lodge

Cocoa Point

Gravenor
Bay

Spanish Point

Caribbean Sea

Dodington Bank

Codrington Shoals

0   1   2   3   4   5

Miles

Morning has broken

The sun, like a huge, ripe orange, rises slowly from behind the Caribbean
sea. Streaks of light – some yellow, others red, yet others brightly white –
strike out across the water, dancing on the peaks of gentle, little waves as
they meander towards a shore still cast in night's receding shadow, but
already exposing beaches of white and golden sands. It is daybreak in
Antigua and Barbuda...and everyday is summer.

As the sun ascends – boldly now, for like the day, it too is fully awake –
its golden glow begins to disappear, yielding to a stunning brightness
which hurls itself across the sea and onto the land. The atmosphere is still
cool, for even though the sun has begun to proclaim its dominion over the
earth, its heat is still young and unable to penetrate the strong, North East
Trade Winds which blow steadily across the sea moderating the
temperature.

In an age old tradition, tiny fishing boats oscillate on the sea, making
their way back to the shore, laden with fish for the morning's market. The
fishermen went out at night knowing that daybreak would lure fish to the
sea's surface in ritual welcome to the radiance of a newborn sun before its
heat forced them to seek cooler waters near the ocean floor. The rhythmic
chug of the fishing boats' small, outboard engines mixes with the louder
roar of bigger engines on jet-skis, motor boats and yachts as those who

cater for visitors begin to prepare their equipment for the day's coterie of
people anxious to make the most of a Caribbean holiday.

Slowly now, people begin to appear: first, young natives of Antigua and
Barbuda – their bodies bristling with health, their muscles well developed
– jogging along the beach and occasionally diving into the water to be
refreshed by its invigorating grip. Visitors too come out in this early
morning light and, with a sense of longing at last fulfilled, immerse
themselves into the sea; stretching out on their backs, relaxing their
muscles, letting tensions dissipate; their faces raised to catch the tingling
touch of the sun's glorious rays.

Birds too are part of the morning's activity. There are 140 species on
Antigua and Barbuda, 90 of which are seen regularly. Some are hunters –
such as the Brown Pelicans skimming along the sea, suddenly plunging
into the water only to rise again abruptly, their morning meal caught in
their beaks. Others flit from tree to tree calling out in song and adding to
the ambiance of nature in all its perfection. The Bananaquit and the Lesser
Antillean Bullfinch, black or grey with a reddish breast are the most
common.

As the sun gains in ascendancy, bathing the land in light, colours come
alive – leaves are now vivid green, flowers – the exotic bougainvillea, the

14

hibiscus and the oleander – are red, yellow, white and even purple.
Coconut trees and other palms, that have stood majestically on the shores
of these islands for decades, climb upwards toward the clear blue sky
dotted only here and there with soft, white clouds. Occasionally either a
very old or a very young palm, responding to pressure from the wind,
arches downwards – but even this curve in its posture has a certain grace,
an attractiveness that speaks not of submission to an unwelcome force,
but of surrender to the allure of nature.

The shores – 365 beaches and coves – are the beginnings of a little bit of
paradise; the same paradise that Christopher Columbus encountered in
1493, when on his second journey to what he called the 'new world', he
saw these lands and named them 'Antigua' and 'Barbuda'.

Geography and prehistory

Antigua is 108 square miles (280 sq km) and Barbuda is 62 square miles (160 sq km). The two islands, along with Redonda 0.6 square miles (1.6 sq km), make up the territory of Antigua and Barbuda. Redonda is uninhabited and there are approximatley 85,000 people on Antigua and 1,500 on Barduda. The last population census was done in the early 1970s so accurate figures are not available.

Man inhabited these islands before Christ was born; it has been established that people of the Meso-Indian age lived on Antigua as far back as 1775 BC at Jolly Beach. They were called the 'Siboney' (stone people). While around 500 BC, nomadic wanderers lived and fished at North Sound, there were no settlements on the island until 35 AD when some Amerindians of the Arawak tribe moved from their home in Venezuela and settled near Indian creek establishing fishing villages, some agriculture and pottery. Around 1200 AD another tribe of Amerindians, the Caribs, also came up the chain of islands from South America. They established settlements in Dominica and St Kitts from where they attacked the Arawaks on Antigua taking their women and children as slaves and murdering the men. They called Antigua, 'Waladli', Barbuda, 'Wa'omoni' and Redonda, 'Ocanamanru'.

The vast majority of Antiguans and Barbudans have never seen

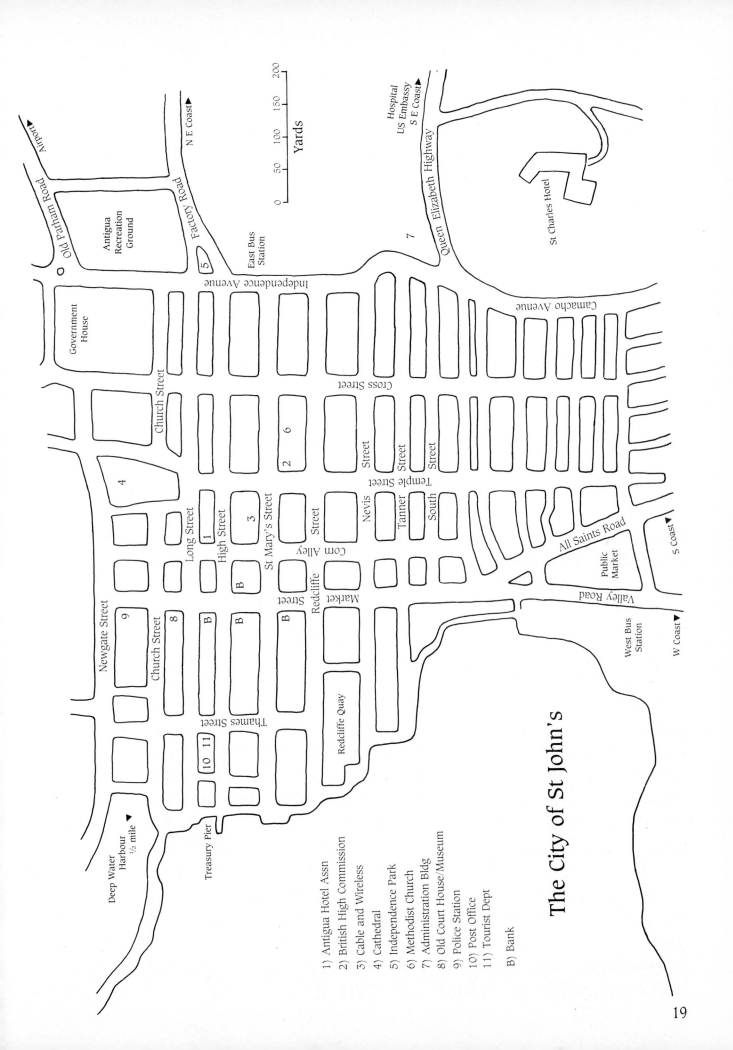

The City of St John's

1) Antigua Hotel Assn
2) British High Commission
3) Cable and Wireless
4) Cathedral
5) Independence Park
6) Methodist Church
7) Administration Bldg
8) Old Court House/Museum
9) Police Station
10) Post Office
11) Tourist Dept

B) Bank

Old Parham Road
Airport
Antigua Recreation Ground
Factory Road
N E Coast
East Bus Station
Independence Avenue
Government House
Church Street
Cross Street
Camacho Avenue
Hospital
US Embassy
S E Coast
Queen Elizabeth Highway
St Charles Hotel
Newgate Street
Church Street
Long Street
High Street
St Mary's Street
Corn Alley
Street
Nevis Street
Temple Street
Tanner Street
South Street
Redcliffe Street
Market Street
All Saints Road
Public Market
Valley Road
S Coast
West Bus Station
W Coast
Thames Street
Redcliffe Quay
Treasury Pier
Deep Water Harbour ½ mile

Yards
0 50 100 150 200

19

(Opposite) The Old
Court House, built in
1747 and rebuilt in
1843

Redonda which has always been an 'isolated, precipitious and forbidding rocky island'. Over the years it has been used in a variety of transient ways, including growing cassava for seafarers on the saddle on the top of the rock, issuing postage stamps and mining phosphates from bird guano. However, it is only as a haven for birds that it remains useful.

But there is a man who claims Redonda as his 'Kingdom'. Jon M Wynne Tyson of Sussex, England, says he is King of this volcanic rock where his only subjects are birds which, tired from flight, light upon it mostly to perform their ablutions before taking off for more beneficial places. Tyson's claim stretches back to 1865 when Matthew Dowdy Shiell sailed by Redonda and, bristling with the pride of recent fatherhood, claimed it as a kingdom for his son. The boy was duly brought to the island and officially proclaimed King Phillipe 1. Upon his death, the throne was bequeathed to the poet, John Gawsworth who appointed several eminent writers such as Dylan Thomas, Ellery Queen, J B Priestly and Lawrence Durrell to various royal positions. Gasworth became King Juan 1 passing the kingdom to Wynne Tyson who declared himself King Juan II. No government of Antigua and Barbuda has yet taken the 'kingdom' seriously since, so far, not even the birds of Redonda have been asked to bend a knee to the royal authority of 'King Juan II'.

A short contemporary history

Antigua was first settled by Europeans in 1632 when the English dispatched a party from their principal West Indian colony, St Kitts, under Captain Edward Warner to take possession of it. Apart from a brief period in 1666 when it was captured by the French, Antigua remained British until its independence on 1 November, 1981. Today the country continues to be a Monarchical state sharing Queen Elizabeth II with Britain as its Head of State. Barbuda used to be a separate British possession – it was formally annexed to Antigua on 1 August, 1860.

The man directly responsible for the link between Antigua and Barbuda was Sir Christopher Codrington who came to Antigua from Barbados in 1674 and established the first large sugar estate, which he named Betty's Hope, after his daughter. Sugar production dominated Antigua until the 1970s, utilising most of the land and leaving a legacy of grave economic problems. But, Codrington also leased Barbuda from the British Crown for an annual fee of 'one fat pig if asked'. It has been suggested that Barbuda was a 'stud farm' on which Codrington bred 'quality slaves'. However, there is no hard evidence to support this claim.

Codrington's success with sugar encouraged other planters and soon there was a proliferation of sugar estates across Antigua. Evidence of this are the sugar mills which can still be seen today strewn around the island.

22

Accompanying the spread of sugar estates was the almost complete annihilation of vegetation. As Gregson Davis put it in 'Antigua Black', 'the evergreen woodland was levelled in a manner as thorough as it was irreversible and short-sighted'. Hence apart from the lush Fig Tree Drive, there is a lamentable absence of forests and woods in Antigua today. But the defacing of the natural beauty of the island was not the only consequence of the wanton destruction of vegetation: drought was the principal result of an absence of trees to attract rainfall. The government has sought to tackle this problem by creating Potswork Dam, a huge man-made lake in the centre of Antigua, and constructing a desalanisation plant to convert sea water for domestic and industrial use.

By 1678, half the island's population consisted of black slaves brought from the West Coast of Africa to cultivate sugar. The harrowing and inhuman system of slavery is well known. Suffice to say that the lot of the black slaves in Antigua was no different from their counterparts in the Caribbean and North and South America – the Antigua slaves were whipped and worked from sun up to sun down; resistance was met with foul punishments including dismembering of the body. Naturally, many rebelled and only musket and shot compelled them to remain the victims of slavery.

24

(Opposite, top)
Shipping sugar at
Willoughby Bay

(Bottom) View near St
John's showing slaves
around their huts with
St John's Cathedral in
the background

The slaves on Antigua were emancipated on 1 August 1834 along with those in The Bahamas and Bermuda. In all of the other British colonies in the Caribbean, there was a 4 year transition period, called apprenticeship, before full freedom was granted. The reason for the immediate emancipation of the Antigua slaves was entirely economic. Since the slaves had no means of earning a living other than by working on the sugar estates, the plantation owners freed them, paid them a derisory wage and evaded the burden of feeding, clothing and housing them.

In the meantime, Barbuda was so little remembered in Britain that the draftsmen of the Bill for the Abolition of Slavery had omitted it in the document. Codrington continued to maintain the former slaves on Barbuda but on 2 April 1860, he wrote a letter addressed to all of them suggesting that they go to work on his estates in Antigua because there was nothing for them to do on Barbuda. They refused. On 1 August 1860, by an Order-in-Council signed by the British Monarch at the Isle of Wight, Barbuda was annexed to Antigua. Neither the Antigua legislature nor the freed slaves on Barbuda were happy with this development – the former because they felt it would be a burden on their treasury and the latter because they disliked Antigua which, over the years had become a place of punishment in their minds since it was there that the unruly among them

were sentenced.

The condition of black people on Antigua and Barbuda was not made
easier after emancipation. They were legally free but, for all practical
purposes, still bound to their plantations. For they had no land on which to
farm and no money with which to establish an independent venture.
Hence, their labour was exploited by the plantation owners.

It is a tribute to their tenacity and industry that in the four years
following emancipation, despite the brutality of slavery from which they
had recently emerged and the deprivation into which they were delivered,
they moved from being landless wage earners to possessors of 1,037
houses in 27 villages. They bought plots of land on hire purchase and met
their payments faithfully. After working a full day on the sugar
plantations, they went home to cultivate their front and back gardens with
plantains, yams, bananas and pineapples. They even found time to grow
flowers. The carefully laid out plots with their pretty gardens can still be
seen today in villages such as Liberta, the first of the free villages to be
created.

Conditions became increasingly intolerable for the workers and by the
Late 1930s, when the bottom dropped out of the economy, Antigua, like
the rest of the West Indies, was ready for change. A Royal Commission,

28

under the Chairmanship of Lord Moyne, was sent out to the region, arriving in Antigua in December 1938. On 1 January, 1939 a member of the Commission, Sir Walter Citrine, addressed a public meeting in the Anglican Cathedral school room in St John's, Antigua's capital. He urged the formation of a trades union to fight for workers' rights.

Among his audience was Vere Conrwall Bird who was elected to the Executive of the Antigua Trades and Labour Union, formed on 16 January, 1939. In the following years, the Union won victory after victory in pursuit of workers rights and justice. In 1943, V C Bird was elected as the Union's President.

Since then, Bird and Antigua have become synonymous for V C Bird has dominated the last 45 years of Antigua and Barbuda's history. He was elected to the legislature in 1946 and given a seat on the Executive Council. In 1951 after much Union agitation, a system of universal adult suffrage was introduced for general elections. The Union selected eight candidates to contest the elections and won all the seats. In 1956, a ministerial system of Government was introduced and again the Union, under V C Bird, won all the seats in the legislature. In 1961 the position of Chief Minister was introduced and the number of seats in the legislature

Exterior of a
boiling house on
Wetheralls Estate in Old
Antigua

increased from 8 to 10 with Barbuda being made a constituency on its
own; previously Barbuda had been attached to St John's. V C Bird became
the first Chief Minister. It was to be the first of many 'firsts'.

In February 1967, Antigua wanted independence from Britain but
succeeded in getting only the status of 'Associated State' – in charge of all
its internal affairs and a measure of its external relations. V C Bird became
the first Premier. Later on 1 November, 1981 as Antigua and Barbuda
attained full independence from Britain, Bird also became the first Prime
Minister.

But, between 1967 and 1981, Antigua and Barbuda experienced a
political upheaval which broke the hold of the Antigua Trades and Labour
Union (AT&LU). In the mid 1950s, opposition to Bird and the Union
emerged amongst the professional and business classes who fielded
candidates in the elections of 1956, 1961 and 1966 but were roundly
defeated at all of them. But, in 1968, the solidarity amongst the working
class, which was the backbone of Bird's strength, ended with the
formation of the Antigua Workers Union (AWU) by disgruntled members
of the AT&LU, led by its former General Secretary, George Walter. In
1970, a new political party, the Progressive Labour Movement, was
created with the strong support of the AWU and in 1971 it won the general

elections. Walter became Premier.

The period of the Walter government coincided with unprecedented high prices for oil which affected tourism to the country and sent its import bills sky-rocketing – the effect was devastating. Few governments, especially new and inexperienced ones, survive such economic ill fortune. But, in addition, Walter's government, in an attempt to eliminate V C Bird and his Antigua Labour Party (ALP), passed objectionable laws to curb the freedom of newspapers and public assembly. These actions, in the midst of an economic crisis, brought fierce reaction from the existing political forces. The 1976 general election returned V C Bird and the ALP to office, but for the first time with an opposition in parliament.

The ALP went on to win the 1980 general election and took Antigua and Barbuda into independence despite protests, at the time, from a number of Barbudan leaders that they wanted 'either separate independence or to remain a colony of Britain'. In the general election of 1984, the ALP again won all the seats on Antigua, routing all the opposition forces. The winner of the sole Barbuda seat in the parliament, Eric Burton, became leader of the one-man opposition. Therefore, dissent in the country now comes from political parties outside parliament – the most vocal of these is the Antigua Caribbean Liberation Movement led by

34

(Opposite, top) Jumby Bay, Long Island

(Bottom) Redcliffe, Quay Downtown, St John's

Leonard 'Tim' Hector. A coalition of the traditional political forces emerged in 1986 as the United National Democratic Party, headed by Dr Ivor Heath.

The central place of sugar in the economy ended in 1972 when the industry was closed down and tourism, which had started as a trickle in 1960, became a flood. Since 1976, Antigua and Barbuda has undergone a conspicuous transformation – the economy has experienced steady growth every year due largely to tourism which has increased by leaps and bounds bringing new and expanded hotels, restaurants, boutiques and, most importantly, jobs.

There are now 3,112 rooms available for tourists in Antigua and Barduda. These range from exclusive hotels such as the magnificent *Coco Point Lodge* on Barbuda and the picturesque *Jumbie Bay* on Long Island to more homely guest houses. *The Royal Antiguan* is the country's largest hotel combining all the elements of an idyllic Caribbean holiday with superb conference facilities. Four hotels now offer casinos for the adventurous tourist willing to chance an arm at roulette or black jack. But, all the hotels offer a variety of water sports including water ski-ing, jet ski-ing and wind surfing. Arrangements are also made for deep sea diving, deep sea fishing or cruises on yachts.

Most hotels have their own tennis courts. Indeed, Antigua has become a popular venue for tennis stars from all over the world who come every year to participate in tennis week when stars, locals and visitors, test their skills against each other. Golf is also a popular sport with visitors and hotels arrange for their guests to play at the sprawling 18-hole *Cedar Valley Golf Club*.

Apart from hotels, a heavy investment has been made in maintaining the tourism infrastructure. 67,412 tourists arrived by air in 1977; the number arriving by air in 1987 had more than doubled to reach 159,207. On Antigua, there is a well-equipped airport with direct connections to Frankfurt, London, Miami, New York and Toronto. In addition, Antigua is the gateway to the Eastern Caribbean and South America with daily flights by the fleet of the Antigua-based Leeward Islands Air Transport (LIAT).

The investment also applies to the deep water harbour in St John's. The modern port facilities easily accommodate huge cargo carriers together with the cavernous passenger cruise ships. In 1977, the number of cruise ship passengers disembarking in Antigua was 35,795; the figure in 1987 had risen to 153,308.

When sugar cane was planted on Antigua, the fields occupied over ninety percent of the land and the cultivation of other crops was

(Opposite) Copper and Lumber Hotel

discouraged by the plantation owners. So, apart from sugar cane, there has been no tradition of large scale agricultural production, particularly as the country's history of drought was unhelpful to farmers. Today, however, a major drive is evident in agricultural production, especially for vegetables. The work is hard, but a system of reservoirs for irrigation and an improved price for produce has encouraged a new interest in the rewards of agriculture. *The Antigua Black*, a small but sweet pineapple, which is one of the national symbols of the country appearing on its Coat of Arms, is now exported as are melons and a variety of vegetables.

The country's economy has also benefited from a good investment climate. Except for a few products, Antigua and Barbuda enjoys duty free access to the market of 11 Commonwealth Caribbean countries, Canada, the United States of America and the countries of the European Economic Community. Manufacturing enterprises, particularly enclave industries exporting to the markets of the USA and Canada, have found a hospitable and helpful environment including duty-free concessions, tax free holidays and a trained and capable work force. Today, industries produce garments, beds and mattresses, paint, electronic equipment, stoves, refrigerators and furniture.

These developments have resulted in more and better jobs for Antiguans

40

(Opposite, top) V.C.
Bird International
Airport handles flights
from all over the world
from Jumbo to micro. In
the foreground (left) is
one of LIAT's aircraft.
LIAT is the Airline of
the Caribbean

(Bottom) Runaway
Beach Hotel

and Barbudans in tourism, agriculture and industry. As a consequence, the standard of living today is higher than at any time in the country's history. And what is very important is that gradually, but appreciably, citizens of Antigua and Barbuda have become owners of an increasing number of productive enterprises, making from their native land their own 'little bit of paradise'....

(Opposite) Government
of Antigua and Barbuda
School Buses

Morning 'till night

From the crack of dawn, the ever present sun reaches into every nook and
cranny of house and hotel waking up sleepy eyes.

But, in the rural areas of Antigua, farmers are up before the sun to
prepare a meal before heading to their lands. These folks are the salt of the
earth; their bodies aged but slim and strong from years of toil; they are god
fearing: gentle despite their strength, mannerly and correct despite their
ruggedness.

Many of them have only small subsistence plots from which, year after
year, they have produced crops for sale in the market place or to the
Government Marketing Corporation. Their enemies do not exist among
men; their foes are pests which threaten their young plants and rains
which seldom come. Some of them rear cattle and, day after day, armed
with a prodding stick and wearing a wide straw hat to shade their heads
from the sun, they walk the land, leading a herd of goats or cows, looking
for good grazing spots.

For the most part, these are older people who have worked to educate
their children and, in doing so, have lost the majority of them from the
land. These same children, now grown up, work in offices and hotels.
They too rise before the sun to catch the buses which leave the countryside
early in the morning to bring passengers to central points in St John's from

44

which they disperse to work. The bus ride is an animated affair – in a
community so small, few are strangers and the journey is filled with
excited conversation and laughter. Occasionally, there is a quarrel, but
even this is a kind of theatre: seldom going beyond the point of loud
voices, the body language of threat and counter threat, so naturally
expressed, could have been choreographed for the stage. Fellow
passengers, like any good audience, fully enjoy a spectacle they know will
go no further than histrionics.

No morning is a morning to lie in bed – not even for the holiday maker.
The greater luxury is to bask on the beach, enjoying the contrasting
sensations of warming sunshine and cooling breeze. But first
breakfast...breakfast in all sorts of combinations, American, European and
West Indian: eggs and bacon, croissant and danish or salted fish. And
what delicious fruits – pineapple, papaw and guava which were here
before Columbus; bananas and oranges brought to the Caribbean by the
Spanish; mango brought from West Africa by the British. The ultimate
luxury in life is to have breakfast against the backdrop of the Caribbean
sea – as blue as all the songs say it is – listening to waves as they amble up
to the shore and gently splash across the hardened sand.

Beach activity is a dazzle of colour in a combination of busy jet skis,

46

catamarans, yachts and billowing sails. Alongside this are vendors, mostly women – some short and buxom, others tall and thin, occasionally a few both tall and buxom. Their summons to buy their wares – colourful dresses, T-shirts, beads, costume jewellery made of local material – are friendly and challenging. The beach bar opens early doing a brisk business in fruit punches for kids and the faint of heart: doing better trade in rum punches for the brave.

The sea has distinctive attractions, best appreciated by snorkelling. The water over the reefs is crystal clear and reveals a colourful marine life with parrot fish, puffers, moray eel and trumpet fish darting this way and that. Deep sea diving, of course, provides a better view of the rich marine life under the sea. Keen fishermen will also find a variety of fish such as Snapper, Grouper, Wahoo, Kingfish and Lobsters which abound in the waters between Antigua and Barbuda.

It is the Antigua waters that every year provide the venue for *Sailing Week*, one of the most sought after events in the yacht racing calendar. And no day during this week is complete without some form of participation in the five gruelling races held every year during the last week of April. Starting off as entertainment for local yachtsmen, in 1964 British Overseas Airways Corporation (now British Airways) donated a

silver cup for the winner of the race between Guadeloupe and Antigua. Encouraged by this acknowledgement, the organisers decided in 1967 to hold three days of racing in three classes: racing, cruising and traditional. Since then, *Sailing Week* has not looked back. From 1968, the number of entries multiplied with yachts from all over the world. Soon entries had to be limited to 150.

The races are a test of skill and endurance, followed avidly by hundreds of visitors, who now flock to Antigua for the event, and thousands of locals, who seize vantage points along the coast, to witness World Champion Yachts rubbing hulls with others less known but just as ambitious. And while *Sailing Week* provides good fun on the sea, it is just as good an opportunity for revelry on shore. End of race beach parties attract sailors and spectators alike in a haze of booze, music and good fellowship. But, much of the shore activities is reserved for the last day when the daring try to walk the greasy pole with many ending up in the sea; men and women join in the nautical tug-o-war quenching their thirst in the beer drinking competition; and the rubber raft race always produces a few sailors rendered legless by more than a few generous tots of rum.

The centre of all this activity is *Nelson's Dockyard* at English Harbour. The dockyard is named after Admiral Lord Horatio Nelson, the British hero

of the Battle of Trafalgar during the Napoleonic wars between England and France. Nelson arrived in Antigua in 1784 at the age of 26 and stayed for three years. The house in which he lived is now a museum. He was Senior Naval Captain at the time in command of a Frigate, *Boreas*. He returned there in 1805 to provision his ship on his way to defeat Villeneuve at Trafalgar and so carve a permanent place for his name in the history books of the world.

But English Harbour's importance preceded Nelson – in the early 1700s, it was selected along with Port Royal in Jamaica as one of the permanent naval stations in the Caribbean. Situated in an old volcano cone, English Harbour is made up of virtually land locked basins with only a narrow passage to the sea – this protected it both from the weather and from sightings from the sea.

It was to defend this naturally strategic location that fortifications were built, between 1780 and 1790, on the overhanging mountain ridges by order of General Thomas Shirley when he became Captain General and Governor in Chief of the Leeward Islands. The ruins of those fortifications at what is now called *Shirley Heights* can still be seen today. There too is *Clarence House* where the Duke of Clarence, later to be King William IV, lived where he served in the Royal Navy.

52

Looking out from Shirley Heights at the panorama of English Harbour, Falmouth Harbour and the broad sweep inland, it is obvious how the country was shorn of its trees – the mountain sides are bare and harsh with only the hardy acacia plants holding the soil together. Throughout the countryside, apart from occasional coconut and breadfruit trees, it is the sturdy acacia with its gnarled branches and yellow blossoms that brings relief to dry and dusty plains.

But, along the coast the perfection of nature in the majestic bays and coves make up for the imperfections of man which led the sugar cane planters to destroy the forest cover of the land. The waters in *Willoughby Bay* and *Half Moon Bay, Mosquito Cove* and *Hawksbill*, run turquoise, green and blue – wondrous spectacles causing even the hardened to catch a breath.

No day is complete without seeing the Capital, St John's. It is congested in a friendly way. For even though most of the shops are tiny and the sidewalks are narrow, there is no feeling of pressure. Life moves on in a laid-back, relaxed atmosphere. The shops are all full to overflowing with stock and the noise of the traffic and conversations is punctuated with the rhythms pouring out of a record store or from a building where a live band

may be rehearsing.

The town started around a Fort whose construction began on Rat Island in 1672. In 1683 the first St John's Church was built and soon the community which moved to the area grew in size. A market was built in 1702 and cross streets were laid out. Then, the institutional buildings were put in place: Government House in 1801 and a General Post Office in 1850. The mid 19th century was a period of great construction activity in St John's following a fire in 1841 which devastated many buildings. The result of different eras of construction has left the town with a blend of architectural styles: Georgian, Victorian, Romantic and International. Now, the St John's redevelopment project has replaced slum areas with buildings which recall the architectural form of the mid 19th century. The panoply of structures are as eye catching collectively as they are significant in their individual representation of ages past and present.

Because Antigua was an important sugar producing island in the 18th and 19th centuries, St John's has always been a busy commercial capital. It is said that, in the mid 19th century, at least twelve ships from London or Liverpool could be seen in the harbour at one time. The town has remained a vibrant commercial centre housing a number of banks, many of them branches of internationally known institutions.

56

St John's also offers restaurants, shopping and historic sites. *The Old Court House* now accommodates the Museum and Archives which serve as a repository for historical documents and as a display centre of the country's history. The building was first erected in 1747 but was damaged in a great earthquake in 1843 and restored. Another earthquake in 1947 damaged it again and it had to be rehabilitated a second time. Nearby is *St John's Cathedral*. Built on the same spot as the original church of 1683, the existing building was consecrated in 1848. Its two towers in a baroque style dominate the skyline.

Not too far away is the Antigua Recreation Ground – venue for Caribbean and international cricket and football matches. Antiguans have been able to watch their own Vivian Richards captain the West Indies Cricket Team to victory there. They have also seen other Antiguans, like Richie Richardson and Curtley Ambrose break into the West Indies Team through natural and graceful talent.

Antigua's national hero, a slave called *Prince Klaass*, who conspired to start a rebellion to set his people free was tortured and killed in 1736 on the very spot where the Antigua Recreation Ground is now located. A body died that day but the spirit which sought freedom lives on and is given expression in *Carnival* in Antigua and *Caribana* in Barbuda when

the rich culture of the two islands are celebrated in a festival of music, song and dance.

Carnival is always during the last week of July and the first week in August coinciding with the anniversary of the abolition of slavery on 1 August 1834. Significantly, the Carnival shows, where the creative spirit of the Antiguan people soars, are held on the same ground in which the planters sought to kill the spirit of freedom which lived in the body of Prince Klaass.

The beauty of the Antiguan and Barbudan people is fully displayed at Carnival and Caribana – it is obvious in the way they stand, their posture relaxed; the easy way in which they laugh; the rhythm of their dance; the unbridled joy in their music and song. And there is a pride in their faces that belies the history of servitude suffered by their forebears.

The costumes for the Queen shows are extravagant; their conception and creation begin at the end of one Carnival show and last to the start of another. The same detailed care goes into the costumes of the troupes which 'play mas' in the streets, dancing behind their favourite band. The 'road march' is chosen by the steelbands from the calypsos performed each year. But, the Calypso competition brings out the true spirit of the Antiguan and Barbudan personality for the calypso performance is theatre

masking serious commentary on social, political and economic ills in the society. No one and nothing is safe from the scathing attention of the calypsonians who, throughout Carnival and Caribana, occupy pride of place in the hearts of the people.

But what a season Carnival and Caribana bring! Music rings out everywhere throughout the periods leading up to scheduled events. By Carnival J'Ouvert morning, people from all walks of life are psyched up for a day of non-stop dancing through the streets, intoxicated with the driving music and the atmosphere of total abandon. There is a deliberate effort to involve children with the Children's Carnival and the Mr and Miss Teenage Pageant Contests – not that they needed encouragement, for officially involved or not, children are ready participants in the joy of life which the festivals bring.

As the sun finally sets on these islands bringing another day to an end and relinquishing its hold to the night, the yachts come home to dock; the beaches give up their guests to the restaurants and nightclubs; offices and factories release their people to nocturnal pursuits. A cool atmosphere descends upon the islands as the sun disappears beyond the sea's horizon. It is the Caribbean moon that now claims dominion, casting a romantic light across the land and onto the waters of the Caribbean and the Atlantic.

Restaurants offering a wide cuisine welcome guests to candlelight and seranading minstrels. The nightclubs start much later and carry on until the small hours of the morning. The bars serve drinks to local and visitors alike. For the adventurous, moonlight cruises on a cool Caribbean sea are also available.

The day has been filled with activity; the night has wound it down gently and a taste has been shared of the 'little bit of paradise' that is Antigua and Barbuda.

(Left) Jolly Beach Hotel

(Opposite, top) Halcyon Hotel

(Bottom) Antigua Village

(Top) Curtain Bluff
Hotel

(Bottom) Dian Bay
Resort

(Opposite) Anchorage
Hotel

(Top) Cocoa Point, Barbuda

(Bottom) Spanish Point, Barbuda

(Opposite, top) The Barrymore Hotel

(Bottom) The Blue Heron

(Left) Warri Pier
Restaurant, Halcyon
Cove

(Opposite) Aerial view
of the Royal Antiguan
Hotel

(Left) Halcyon Cove
Hotel

(Opposite) Fort
Barrington on top of
Goat Hill

74

(Left) Para-sailing with Sea Sports, at Dickenson Bay

(Opposite, top) The Lord Nelson Club (Hotel)

(Bottom) Hodges Bay Club (Hotel)

(Top) The Beachcomber
Hotel

(Bottom) Antigua Sugar
Mill (Hotel)

(Opposite) Catamaran
Marina, Falmouth

(Left) The Royal Antiguan

(Opposite, top) The Royal Antiguan Resort and Casino

(Bottom) Trev-T-Bone Resort

(Top) The Inn at English Harbour

(Bottom) Dian Bay Resort

(Opposite, top) Antigua Village

(Bottom) Blue Heron Hotel

(Top) Copper and Lumber Hotel

(Bottom) Catamaran Hotel

(Opposite, top) Buccaneer Cove

(Bottom) Sunset View Hotel, Barbuda

(Top) Falmouth Beach
Apartments

(Bottom) Galleon Beach
Club

88

(Top) Jolly Beach Hotel

(Bottom) Long Bay Hotel

(Opposite) Pineapple Beach Hotel

90

(Left) Anchorage Hotel

(Opposite, top) Siboney Beach Club

(Bottom) Sandpiper Reef

(Top) Blue Waters Hotel

(Bottom) Sand Haven Hotel

(Opposite, top) Barrymore Hotel

(Bottom) Barrymore Beach Apartments

(Left) East coast, Barbuda

(Opposite, top) Sunset at Dickenson Bay

(Bottom) Sunset at Codrington, Barbuda

(Left) Moonrise at St James Club

(Opposite) For the most spectacular sunset view on English Harbour from Lookout Restaurant

(Left) The courtyard at Admirals Inn

(Opposite) Peace and tranquillity on one of Antigua's many superb beaches

(Left) Hunting for welks at Spanish Point

(Opposite) Hawksbill Rock inspired the naming of the nearby Hawksbill Hotel

(Left) Beach cricket using a coconut bough for a bat

(Opposite) "Rastaman" shaking his dreadlocks

104

(Top) Sandy Island houses a navigation beacon for entry to St John's Harbour. The reefs surrounding the island also provide excellent scuba diving and snorkelling activities

(Bottom) Beach near Jolly Beach Hotel in Lignumvitae Bay

(Opposite, top) The view of Morris Bay

(Bottom) Fishing with a line and no rod

(Top) Getting a snack from the "lunch lady"

(Bottom, and opposite top) Happy school children in Barbuda

(Bottom) Local fishermen taking time out for a drink during Barbuda's Caribana celebrations

(Top) Rural Antigua

(Bottom) Westindies oil refinery, Friars Hill

(Opposite, top) A US Marine dropping in with the Antigua and Barbuda national flag during Independence celebrations

(Top) Antigua and Barbuda Parliament building was officially opened by H.R.H. Princess Margaret, who delivered the first Throne Speech in the newly independent country on 1st November 1981

(Bottom) The headquarters of the Ministry of Foreign Affairs, Economic Development, Tourism and Energy

(Opposite, top) Inside Parliament, the Minister of Finance, The Honourable John E. St. Luce delivers the budget speech

(Bottom) Parliament is opened with full ceremony by Her Majesty the Queen's representative Sir Wilfred Jacobs, Governor-General

(Left) November 1st is Antigua and Barbuda's Independence Day, marked every year with a solemn ceremony

(Opposite, top) Local dignitaries at the celebration of Antigua and Barbuda's anniversary of Independence (Prime Minister Rt. Hon Dr. V.C. Bird is third from left in the front row)

(Bottom) The Governor-General inspecting the Guard-of-Honour at the opening of Parliament

(Left) Independence Day Parade at the recreation ground

(Opposite) The Governor-General taking the salute

116

117

(Left and opposite)
Strike up the band for
Independence Day

(Left) On parade

(Opposite) The National Majorettes

(Left) Talent segment of the Miss Teenage Pageant

(Opposite) Displaying locally designed and manufactured casual wear

(Left) Telling it like it is – Barbudian calypsonian, Golden Locks

(Opposite) Not calypso, but entertaining all the same

(Left) Antiguan beauty, combining fashion with elegance

(Opposite) Dancing in paradise

126

(Left) Exotic Carnival costume in street parade

(Opposite) Young Majorette

(Top) The Parade of Troupes

(Opposite) Carnival Queen contestant in full regalia

(Bottom) Part of the Carnival celebrations – J'Ouvert Morning

(Opposite) A 'Mr Teenage Pageant' contestant

(Top) Dance performed by students of Christ The King High School

(Bottom) Spectators at the judging of Troupes and Groups at the Antigua Recreation Grounds

(Opposite) King Short Shirt – 25 years as a calypsonian and still going strong

(Top) A familiar sight at the opening of Carnival City – The reigning Prince and Princess of the Band

(Opposite) Carnival Queen contestant

136

(Top) Everyone gets involved at Carnival

(Bottom) Antiguan dancer performing at Barbuda's Caribana

(Opposite) J'Ouvert Morning 'Jump-up'

(Top) Parade of troupes

(Bottom) A member of the 'Burning Flames' – Antigua's no.1 party band

(Opposite) Carnival Queen contestant

140

(Top) A wave from a hopeful Carnival Queen contestant

(Bottom) The attraction is 'Burning Flames'

(Opposite) The judging of Troupes and Groups on stage at Carnival City

(Left) The talent spot during the Carnival Queen contest

(Opposite) Carnival Queen contestant in evening wear

(Left) A contestant of the popular Mr Teenage Pageant

(Opposite) Carnival is fun for everyone

(Left) Carnival Queen
contestant displaying
her talents

(Opposite) One of the
many splendid
costumes displayed at
Carnival.

148

(Top) Sunday afternoon entertainment at The Lookout restaurant

(Bottom) Carnival

(Opposite) Miss Barbuda, Caribana Queen

(Opposite) A fashion show at Feathers nightclub which is organised by local designers using local models

(Top) First day celebrations during Antigua Sailing Week at Dickenson Bay

(Bottom) Another event during Antigua Sailing Week – the Wet Tee-Shirt contest at the Antigua Yacht Club

(Opposite) Antigua Sailing Week attracts entrants from all over the world. This one is Kialoa IV, from the United States

(Top) Sunday afternoon at the Lookout – a most popular viewpoint

(Bottom) One of the Antigua Sailing Week races

(Opposite) The Ting Windsurfing and Sailing Regatta held in the last weekend of January

(Top) Beer drinking
contest at the Antigua
Yacht Club during the
Lay Day celebrations

(Bottom) Preparations
for the Greasy Pole
Competition

(Opposite) Not quite
"walking the greasy
pole" on Dockyard Day

(Top) The Non-Mariners Race is for anything that floats

(Bottom) Just!

(Opposite) Stars of the Non-Mariners Race

160

(Top) The Non-Mariners Race during Sailing Week

(Bottom) There's more than one use for a sail bag at the Lay Day Games

(Opposite, top) Just hitching a ride

(Bottom) Start of the Antigua & Barbuda Triathalon – now an annual event and attracting international competitors

(Top) Laser Racing at the Ting Windsurfing and Sailing Regatta

(Bottom) Antigua Sailing Week

(Opposite) The Female Deciduous Legs Competition at the Antigua Yacht Club

(Top) Dockyard Day
celebrates the end of
Sailing Week with
parties and prize-giving

(Bottom) Sun fish
racing at the Ting
Windsurfing and Sailing
Regatta

(Opposite, Top) View of
Nelson's Dockyard from
Shirley Heights

(Bottom) Presentation
of prizes to the winners
of events during
Antigua Sailing Week

(Top) More than 40 pounds of wahoo coming aboard from Antigua's deep sea

(Opposite) The pleasure is in the catch. Here is 225 pounds of blue marlin pleasure caught by the crew of Rimora

(Top) "Could you believe that we caught all this fish and still didn't win!"

(Bottom) The champion sports fishing boat, Realitie, with its prize-winning catch

(Opposite) Close up of a anemone

171

(Top) Spiny puffer fish

(Bottom) Red hind

(Opposite) Diver holding a spiny puffer fish

172

(Top) A school of yellow tailed snappers

(Bottom) A coney

(Opposite, top) Black bar soldier fish

(Bottom) French angel fish

Just a few of the many tropical fish found at Antiguan dive sites

(Top) Spotted moray eel

(Bottom) Young lobster emerging from coral formation

(Opposite) A trumpet fish

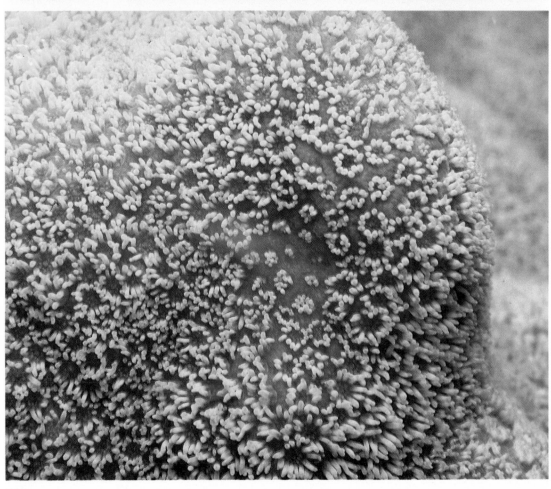

179

(Top) Red hibiscus

(Opposite) Pink
hibiscus

182

(Top) Poinsettia

(Bottom) Yellow bells

(Opposite, top) Crotons

(Bottom)
Bougainvillaea

184

185

(Bottom) Cactus

(Opposite) Top of a cactus

186

(Top) Young cactus plants

(Bottom) The rugged east coast of Barbuda

188

(Top) The roads are for everyone and everything

(Opposite, top) Having taken the horse to water...

(Bottom) In Codrington, Barbuda's capital, one horse-power will do for transportation

(Bottom) Coconut grove outside Codrington, Barbuda's capital

(Top) In this paradise, Eve tempts Adam with a coconut

(Bottom) J'Ouvert morning during carnival a welcome drink of coconut water

(Opposite) Two Foot Bay on the rugged east coast of Barbuda

(Top) Ruins near Two Foot Bay, Barbuda

(Bottom) The "Antigua Black" pineapple is the national fruit of Antigua and Barbuda. This plantation is near Cades Bay

(Opposite) A yellow crowned night heron

196

(Left) A great egret

(Opposite) Terns

(Left) A baby frigate bird in the bird sanctuary, Barbuda

(Opposite, top) Young frigate birds at play. Although they now have a wing span of nearly three feet they are still unable to fly

(Bottom) A great egret in the breeding season

(Left) Frigate bird sancturary, Barbuda

(Opposite) Brown pelicans

202

(Left) The beautiful and peaceful beach at Spanish Point, Barbuda

(Opposite, top) Black birds sharing breakfast with a turtle dove.

(Bottom) A black winged stilt

(Left) The beach at Ffryes Bay

(Opposite, top) A healthy brood of chicks

(Bottom) Scuba divers returning to base.

(Left) The Roman Catholic Church at Tyrells

(Opposite) The entrance to St. John's Cathedral. The life-size metal figures, representing St. John the Baptist and St. John the Divine are believed to have been taken from a French ship captured during the Seven Years War (1756-1763)

(Left) Our Lady of the Valley Church in the parish of St. Mary's

(Opposite) On Good Friday Catholics re-enact the Stations of the Cross from the village of All Saints to the Church at Tyrells

(Left) The interior of St. John's Cathedral, which seats about 2000 people, is completely encased in pine timber so as to lessen the effects of earthquakes

(Opposite) St Peter's Church at Parham

(Top) Pilgrim Holiness Church, Codrington, Barbuda

(Bottom) Christ the King High School Choir

(Opposite) A fish-eye view of St. John's Cathedral which was re-built in 1847. The twin towers are one of the landmarks in the city of St. John's

214

(Left) The King in his Kingdom. Viv Richards, captain of the Westindies Cricket Team and internationally renowned batsman, at home in Antigua

(Opposite) Spectators at the Pakistan/Westindies cricket match

217

(Left) Curtley Ambrose about to let loose with a thunderbolt

(Opposite, top) Cricket in the ideal setting of Old Road

(Bottom) Cedar Valley 18 hole golf course

219

(Left) Antigua's number one female golfer, Louise Baretto

(Opposite) Agony or joy; a miss or a hole?

(Left) Premier Division football at the Antigua Recreation Grounds

(Opposite, top) A panoramic view from Cedar Valley golf course

(Bottom) Sports day at St. Joseph's Academy

(Left) Antigua and Barbuda's national football team, in yellow, playing against Dominica's national team at the Antigua Recreation Grounds

(Opposite) Horse-racing at Casada Gardens Turf Club

(Left) Volunteers providing refreshments to the athletes during the cycling leg of the annual Triathalon

(Opposite) Cruising the Caribbean waters with a cool breeze behind you. Who could ask for anything more?

(Top) Antigua's waters provide excellent conditions for all levels of water sports, from beginner to professional

(Bottom) A water sports mecca for all. A tranquil west coast and windy east coast provide the variety to meet the needs of most water sports

(Opposite) Windsurfing is probably the fastest growing sport in Antigua attracting locals as well as tourists. Lessons for beginners and equipment for all levels of skill are available at most of the hotels and at some private water sports' operators

(Left) Windsurfing at the Lord Nelson Club on the north-east coast provides a variety of sailing conditions – from gentle breezes to gusts suitable for wave jumping.

(Opposite) On windy days Half Moon Bay provides ideal conditions for high speed sailing and wave jumping as Xabier Ross demonstrates here.

(Left) A glass bottom boat picking up passengers from Blue Waters Hotel

(Opposite, top) Galleon Beach Club

(Bottom) Halcyon Cove

(Left) Para-sailing at Dickenson Bay with Sea Sports

(Opposite, top) A water sport where one need not get wet

(Bottom) Inigo Ross, Antigua's top water-skier

235

(Top) Ruins of Betty's Hope Estate presently being restored

(Bottom and opposite) Martello Tower situated on the south coast of Barbuda, overlooking what used to be the main landing place 'The River'. The reason for the use of this name is unclear as no river has ever existed anywhere on Barbuda

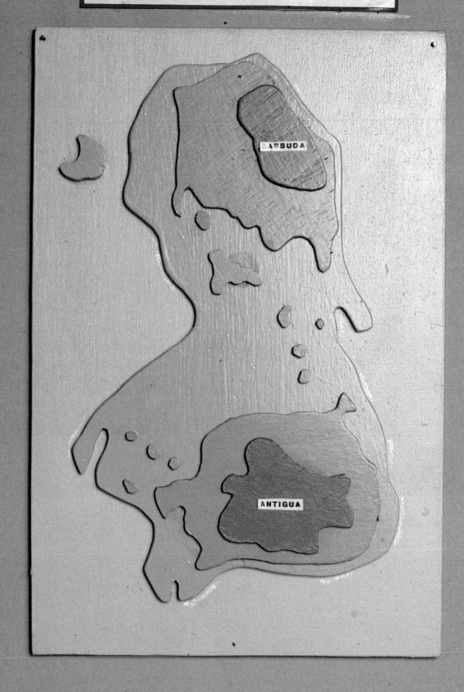

ANTIGUA AND BARBUDA CONNECTED AT 10,000 BC

BARBUDA

ANTIGUA

ANTIGUA AND BARBUDA SEPARATED ABOUT 9,600 BC

GLACIAL ICE OF THE PLEISTOCENE PERIOD BEGAN TO MELT ABOUT 10,000 BC OR 12,000 YEARS AGO AND THE SEALEVEL ROSE

(Left) Part of a display on the geology of Antigua and Barbuda at the museum in St. John's

(Opposite) Officers' quarters and barracks at Shirley Heights dating back to 1791

238

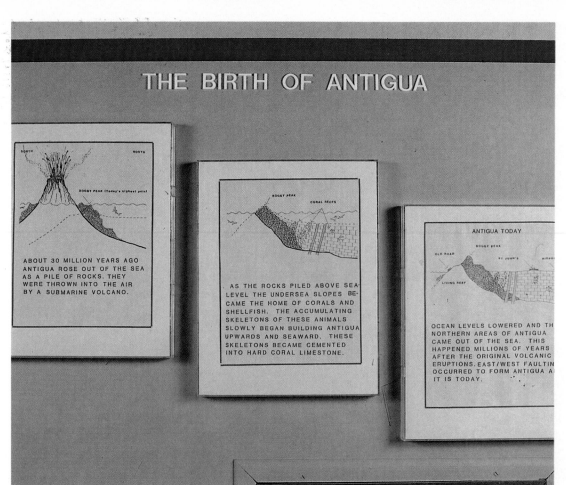

THE BIRTH OF ANTIGUA

ABOUT 30 MILLION YEARS AGO ANTIGUA ROSE OUT OF THE SEA AS A PILE OF ROCKS. THEY WERE THROWN INTO THE AIR BY A SUBMARINE VOLCANO.

AS THE ROCKS PILED ABOVE SEA-LEVEL THE UNDERSEA SLOPES BECAME THE HOME OF CORALS AND SHELLFISH. THE ACCUMULATING SKELETONS OF THESE ANIMALS SLOWLY BEGAN BUILDING ANTIGUA UPWARDS AND SEAWARD. THESE SKELETONS BECAME CEMENTED INTO HARD CORAL LIMESTONE.

OCEAN LEVELS LOWERED AND TH NORTHERN AREAS OF ANTIGUA CAME OUT OF THE SEA. THIS HAPPENED MILLIONS OF YEARS AFTER THE ORIGINAL VOLCANIC ERUPTIONS. EAST/WEST FAULTIN OCCURRED TO FORM ANTIGUA A IT IS TODAY.

(Left) The museum – St. John's

(Opposite) 1736 the slave Prince Klass attempted to blow up the plantocracy at the governors' ball

240

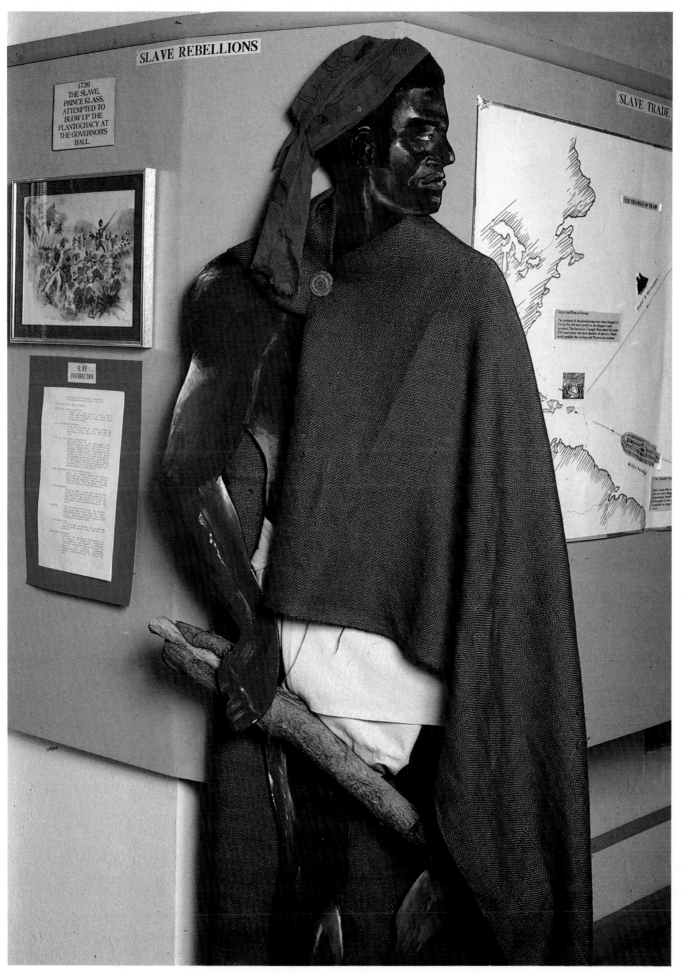

SLAVE REBELLIONS

(Left) The Old Court House, built in 1747, now houses the Antigua & Barbuda Museum on the ground floor and the Archives on the first floor. It is one of the oldest buildings still in use in St. John's. Definitely worth a visit.

(Opposite) Old sugar mill at Dunbars. Surrounded by beautiful flowers, it is a treat for photographers

242

(Left) Built in the early eighteenth century the cannons at Fort Berkeley still command the entrance into Nelson's Dockyard

(Opposite) Located at the bottom of Redcliffe Street, in St John's, is this plaque dedicated to the memory of Dr. Thomas Coke, "Father of the Methodist Missionary Society" who landed there on December 25th, 1786

245

(Top) Fort James, built in the early 18th century to protect the harbour at St. John's, still affords a lovely view of the harbour. Many of its old cannons and walls are still intact and definitely worth a visit.

(Bottom) Clarence House, originally built for Prince William Henry, Duke of Clarence, in 1787, is now the official country residence of the Governor-General. When he is not in residence, the house is open to the public. Guided tours are provided and are very entertaining

(Opposite) Driving through the countryside, one is made conscious of the remnants of our plantation days and of the progress made since

(Left) The War Memorial, situated at Independence Avenue, pays tribute to the Antiguan servicemen who lost their lives during World War I and World War II

(Opposite) Planted by Her Majesty Queen Elizabeth II in Nelson's Dockyard

(Top) Model of an Arawak village which forms a large display in the museum in St. John's

(Bottom) Lord Nelson's house, located in the dockyard, now houses a small souvenir shop and a museum displaying items of the period

(Opposite) Top quality facilities manned by local and foreign doctors and nurses, provide first class medical treatment for those who need it

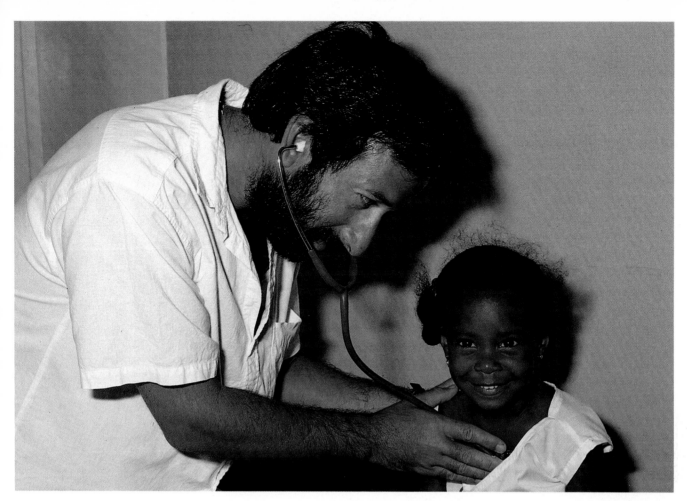

The future of Antigua and Barbuda is in the hands of our youth. We must educate them and provide for all their needs if our country is to continue on its road to greater prosperity for all

(Top) Always ready for duty, the coast guard cutter "Liberta"

(Bottom) Cruise liners docked at St. John's Harbour

(Opposite, top) Locally built boats, used for fishing and for carrying cargo between the islands

(Bottom) Fishing boat loaded with fish pots and ready to go to sea.

(Top) The Yacht Club

(Bottom) Crabbs Marina

(Opposite, top) Cruiser in St John's Harbour

(Bottom) Leaving St John's

258

(Top) Day trips and fishing trips around the island or picnic cruises to outlying islands are available on fast modern boats

(Bottom) View of St John's from Michaels Mount

(Opposite, top) Pelican Island, near Blue Heron Hotel

(Bottom) The Pillars of Hercules seen from the sea

(Top) Hawksbill Beach Hotel, four beaches – one where clothes are optional

(Opposite, top) Devil's Bridge viewed from the sea

(Bottom) The beach at Curtain Bluff

(Opposite, top) Tourists and taxis at Clarence House

(Bottom) Approaching St John's by air

(Top) Basket weaving by the roadside

(Bottom) Sandmining in Barbuda

(Opposite, top) Industry. This factory manufactures local hero Viv Richards' shirts

(Bottom) Furniture making to meet local needs

266

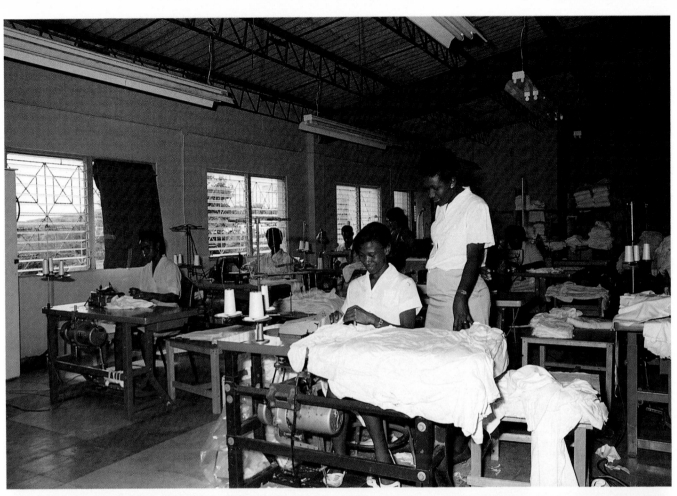

Caribbean style homes

(Opposite) Unique conversion from an old sugar mill to a modern apartment

(Top) Downtown St John's

(Bottom) Redcliffe St, St John's

(Opposite, top) Redcliffe Quay contains many converted shops, stores and restaurants

(Bottom) Market St, St John's

(Left, top) Downtown
supermarkets

(Bottom) The meat
market, St John's

(Opposite) A breadfruit
tree

(Left) Paw-paw

(Opposite) Local fruit
and vegetables

274

(Left) St Josephs Academy students relax after school

(Opposite) St Phillips Church, cemetery and rectory

(Left) Modern communication systems keep Antigua and Barbuda in touch worldwide

(Opposite, top) Putting the finishing touch to a Sealy mattress

(Bottom) The container port at the Deepwater Harbour

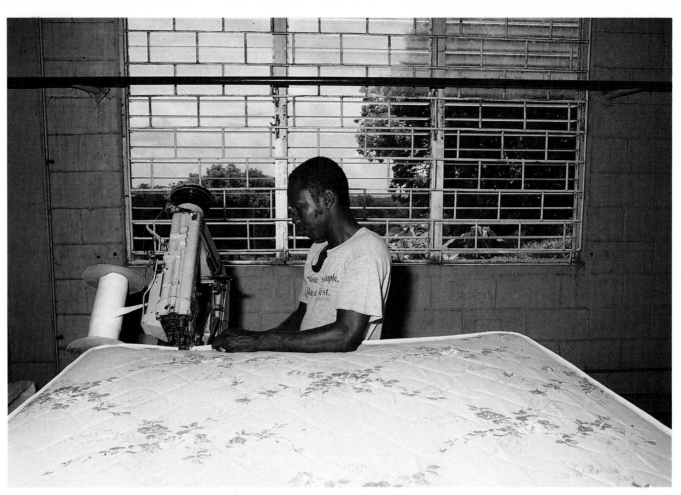

(Left) Basket-making

(Opposite, top) Antigua's desalination plant provides an adequate water supply all year round.

(Bottom) The south coast provides a remarkable contrast and adds variety on trips around the island

280

(Left, top) Carlisle Bay provides yacht anchorage

(Bottom) Lush fruit trees along Fir Tree Walk

(Opposite) Fig Tree Drive and the rain forest

(Left, top) Josephs Supperette

(Bottom) Coates Cottage. Local arts and crafts on display and for sale

(Opposite, top) Take a trip on a glass bottom boat and see the beautiful reefs and marine life. Most boats cater for snorkellers

(Bottom) Aerial shot of Willoughby Bay

(Left, top)
Developments in St
John's

(Bottom) Body Pond
near Swetes Village

(Left, top) Antigua Commercial Bank

(Bottom) A taxi

(Opposite, top) Local taxi drivers playing warri a game unique to the islands

(Bottom) The market place, Downtown, St John's

(Left, top) Aerial view of Potworks dam

(Bottom) Driving through the countryside

(Opposite, top) Perfect anchorage at Green Island, just off the south-east coast of Antigua

(Opposite, bottom) Rugged coastline near the entrance to Deep Bay

(Left, top) Pond near
Monks Hill

(Bottom) A safe landing

(Opposite, top) Fish fry
on the beach

(Bottom) Buckleys
Village

(Left, top) Antigua's 'Black' pineapple

(Bottom) Tropical drink in coconut

(Opposite, top) A cooling spray at Devil's Bridge

(Bottom) A more welcome choice of cooling drinks at Feathers Nightclub

(Left, top) Tennis professionals at Half-Moon Bay tournament, usually early January each year

(Bottom) The courts and climate are ideal for the game

(Left, top) A multitude of little coves and inlets along with private beaches provide perfect anchorage and picnic facilities

(Bottom) Exploring the Caribbean waters in style in the Aquanaut Dive Boat from the Royal Antiguan

(Opposite) International sportsman – local hero Viv Richards captain of the Westindies Cricket Team

(Left, top) Lovely undeveloped beaches are a particular feature of the south-west coast accessible only by boat

(Bottom) Sunset at Hawksbill Rock